every teenager's
little black book
for athletes

by blaine bartel

every teenager's
little black book
for athletes

by blaine bartel

Harrison House
Tulsa, Oklahoma

14 13 12 11   15 14 13 12 11 10 9

Every Teenager's Little Black Book for Athletes
ISBN 13: 978-1-57794-622-9
ISBN 10: 1-57794-622-7
Copyright © 2004 by Blaine Bartel
P.O. Box 691923
Tulsa, Oklahoma 74179

Published by Harrison House, Inc.
P.O. Box 35035
Tulsa, Oklahoma 74153

contents

contents (continued)

Team

Game Day

contents (continued)

Sportsmanship

3 THINGS FREESTYLE SKIING TAUGHT ME

When I was a teenager growing up in Canada, I fell in love with snow skiing. It wasn't long before I was attempting a wide range of aerial acrobatics, including 720°s, front somersaults with full twists, and the nearly-impossible-to-land double-front somersault. I eventually accomplished my goal of winning the gold medal in a provincial competition. Along the way, I learned 3 valuable lessons.

1. **The Reward of Risk.** I discovered the importance of launching out and being willing to take carefully calculated risks in order to win. I'm not talking about the kind of risk that is almost assured to fail, but risks you truly believe you can accomplish that others may hesitate to attempt.

2. **The Value of Vision.** Before you can ever attempt something great, you must see yourself doing it in

your heart and mind. The Bible tells us that without a vision, people perish. (Prov. 29:18 KJV.) Before I would ever physically attempt a jump of any kind, I would see myself successfully landing that jump dozens of times in my imagination.

3. **The Importance of Creativity.** In freestyle skiing, you are always creating. New jumps. Variations of existing maneuvers. Judges and crowds always love to watch something they haven't seen before. Great athletes and great people understand the power of creativity. Never let your opponents think they have you figured out!

4 PRINCIPLES I LEARNED FROM JUDO

Judo is a combat sport, but it is primarily based on defending yourself rather than seeking to attack. Starting this discipline at a very young age, I would eventually become a provincial champion in several weight classes. I loved the challenge of going one on one with an opponent. If you lost, you had only yourself to blame. But when you won, you stood alone on the winner's podium with a tremendous sense of achievement. There are principles I learned in this sport that I have carried throughout my life.

1.   **Respect.** I was taught by my instructor and coach, Yosh Senda, to always show proper respect to an opponent. We would give a traditional bow before each match and shake hands at the end. Never underestimate any battle!

2. **Humility.** Whenever I would come home from a tournament with another first place trophy in tow, the next practice I would be asked to fight an opponent in a higher weight class and a superior belt level. This was a reminder from my coach that there was still work to be done.

3. **Counter.** Much of the time, Judo is being able to effectively counter your attacker, using their offensive maneuver to expose a weakness. I've learned that in difficult, challenging times that you can uncover strengths and opportunities you would have never before realized you had.

4. **Patience.** Many matches would go multiple rounds. If you tried to do too much too quickly at the beginning of the fight, you would sacrifice your stamina needed at the end. I've learned to be patient in waiting

for the right times to make your critical moves in both sports and life.

3 SECRETS I DISCOVERED PLAYING FOOTBALL

I absolutely love football. In my first year of high school football, I became the leading tackler of my team. That year we lost by 3 points in the city championship game. Today I still play pick up games with my friends at work and religiously follow my favorite team, the Dallas Cowboys. Football is a great teacher of character and teamwork. Here are a few secrets I picked up along the way.

1. **Mental make up.** Players who succeed on the gridiron believe they own every field they walk onto. You must be able to look into the eyes of any opponent and truly believe you are better and will dominate them. There is no room for doubt and fear on the field or in life. Confidence is a must!

2. **Great coaching.** I told you how we went to the city championship one year. Did I tell you the next year we

failed to win even one game?! For the most part, we had many of the same players. The difference? A new coach who did a poor job. Winning starts at the top. That's why it's so important that you choose carefully the people who are influencing you. You may not be able to always choose who coaches you, but you are able to choose your employer, your pastor, and your mentors in life. Choose these people well.

3. **Tendencies.** Playing cornerback on defense, I studied the body language of the receivers, the line, even the quarterback. Soon you would discover little tendencies that would let you know if the play was going to be a run or a pass. A lineman who was slightly back on his heels would signal a pass play. The way a receiver would take off at the snap of the ball could tip you to the play called. As in football, it is important to carefully study areas of your personal life

or career, so that you can make decisions that produce the results you want.

4 CHARACTERISTICS HOCKEY GAVE ME

I am a great hockey player in Tulsa, Oklahoma, where I live today. I was a very average hockey player growing up in my native Canada. Just telling an opponent in Tulsa that you grew up playing hockey in Canada gives you instant respect. You have a mental edge before you even take the ice. Here are some great habits hockey gave me.

1. **Toughness.** We used to play on a lake near our house in temperatures sometimes below -25° Fahrenheit. We would have 5 layers of clothes on and a huge scarf wrapped around our face so that only our eyes were exposed to the frigid air. (Even your eyes would be quivering!) But we'd tough it out, play for hours, and love it! Life doesn't always provide perfect conditions. So what! Do it anyways.

2. **Self-control.** At times, opponents would take pretty good swipes at your legs, arms, even head with the shaft of their hockey stick. It not only hurt, but it made you mad. Exercising self-control by not retaliating would put them in the penalty box and you on the power play. Control your emotions.

3. **100%.** As a player, a hockey shift may put you on the ice for 1-2 minutes max, and then you would give way to another line of players. This taught me to give 100% every time I was on the ice. Give your all in all you do.

4. **Sacrifice.** There were many times when an opponent would wind up for a slap shot, and I would slide in front of his shot to stop it from ever getting to our net. If it hit an area of your body unprotected by equipment, holy cow did it hurt! But this was expected as a complete player. Your willingness to make sacrifices that

help further the cause of others will go a long ways in

making you a better person.

5 GOOD HABITS THAT WILL
MAKE YOU A WINNER

1. **Preparation.** "I will do all I must before, so that I can enjoy the results after."

2. **Action.** "I will do what I need to do right now because tomorrow may be too late."

3. **Prayer.** "I realize that my destiny is too great for me to attempt alone. God will be my constant help and source of strength to fulfill my dreams and achieve my destiny."

4. **Character.** "I will live life with honesty and integrity, the kind of attributes that will not just get me to the top, but keep me there."

5. **Discipline.** "I will continue to do what it takes to succeed, even when the excitement has swindled, the new has worn off, and things become routine."

[BELIEVE]

3 REASONS YOUR THOUGHTS WILL
AFFECT YOUR PERFORMANCE

If you've ever been at a great height and had someone tell you, "Don't look down!" then you already understand this concept: You will focus on and be drawn towards what you allow to dominate your thoughts. These are 3 reasons your thoughts will affect your performance.

1. **Your thoughts before a competition establish your image of the event, your team, and your performance.** By focusing your thoughts on the game plan, you begin the process of winning before you ever step on the field.

2. **Your thoughts will determine your level of success in difficult circumstances.** If you let fear or anxiety dominate your thoughts, you move the game from the playing surface into your mind by allowing

fear of failure to make you freeze or keep you from trying again after a mistake.

3. **A disciplined mind allows you to move past distractions and focus on the task at hand.** It is difficult to win in sports, so thinking about the way someone is officiating the event or who is watching can make an uphill climb even harder.

4 WAYS TO INCREASE CONFIDENCE

Confident athletes are successful athletes. In a team environment, confidence can be very contagious. So, here are 4 ways to increase your confidence and become more contagious around your team.

1. **Practice.** If you don't practice and practice hard, it can be almost impossible to have the confidence in your ability or in your team that it takes to win. If you invest time and energy in a practice setting, you will get tremendous returns when game time rolls around.

2. **Prepare.** Practice will get you ready physically, but preparation is also mental. Play through your game or match in your head. Go over your responsibilities and see yourself succeeding. You can be confident as you perform, because you know that you have done

everything possible prior to game time to compete at your best.

3. **Set individual goals.** As you prepare for each practice, game, or season, set several small goals. Whether it is a better time in an event or a certain skill you want to improve, as you work toward and achieve these short-term goals, you will gain confidence in your ability to achieve your long-term goals.

4. **Learn from mistakes.** Whether it is your mistakes or the mistakes of someone else, if you learn what went wrong, you can have confidence as you learn what to do differently next time.

6 THINGS YOU MUST BELIEVE
ABOUT YOURSELF

You will eventually become a product of what you believe. All great athletes, presidents, pastors, and corporate CEOs arrived where they are because they believed they could before anyone else believed in them. Here are 6 things you must believe about yourself.

1. I have been given power over the devil. (1 John 4:4.)

2. I have been given power over every circumstance in my life. (Mark 11:23.)

3. I have a strong body that has been healed by the stripes taken on Jesus' back. (Matt. 8:17.)

4. I have the ability to control my mind and cast out evil thoughts. (2 Cor. 10:4,5.)

5. I am poised for success and will not accept any defeat as final. (1 Cor. 15:57.)

6. I hate sin but love all people and have favor everywhere I go. (Prov. 12:2.)

3 THOUGHTS YOU MUST KEEP OUT

If your thoughts affect your focus and your focus determines your direction, then here are 3 thoughts that you must keep out so you can keep moving in the right direction.

1. **"What if I fail?"** Don't spend your time thinking about failure; think about what it takes to win. Allowing yourself to think about failure makes the event about how you will look or whom you will let down instead of being about the competition itself.

2. **"What do others think about me?"** Fans and spectators will always have contrasting opinions. But, good or bad, the opinions of other people cannot score points or win races. If you practice hard, keep your character strong, and always give your best effort, the results will speak for themselves.

3. **"What about my past?"** Whether you have missed your mark one time or 100 times, dwelling on that will only keep you from reaching it again. Replace those thoughts by thinking about how good it will be to succeed or setting a personal reward for each achievement.

4 DIFFERENCES BETWEEN CONFIDENCE AND ARROGANCE

From a distance, arrogance can easily be mistaken for confidence. Here are 4 marks that make even the most confident person want to keep their distance from arrogance.

1. Confidence is based on a belief that whether I perform well or badly, I will be able to do whatever is next. Arrogance is based on appearance and performance and quickly dissolves in difficult circumstances.

2. Arrogance knows everything and refuses to be coached, even by the most knowledgeable person on even the smallest detail. Confidence is focused on continuing to improve and learning how to do better what you already do well.

3. Confidence means believing in yourself as you make the team better or strive to reach your goals. Arrogance is focused on yourself as you use the team or personal achievements to make yourself look better.

4. Arrogance treats the failures of others as catastrophic mistakes that you would never make. Confidence is using your talents and knowledge to make other athletes better, not to make them feel smaller.

[PREPARATION]

7 PERSONAL BELIEFS THAT WILL
ALTER YOUR FUTURE

Without a doubt, the most important thing you can establish in your life right now is what you believe. Your core convictions will separate you from the pack.

1. I believe I am God's child and He is my Father. (1 John 3:1.)

2. I believe the Holy Spirit leads me in all my decisions. (Rom. 8:14.)

3. I believe I am more than a conqueror in every challenge life brings. (Rom. 8:37.)

4. I believe God is the author of my promotion in every area of life. (Ps. 75:6,7.)

5. I believe that when I pray, God hears me and answers me. (Mark 11:24.)

6. I believe that as I meditate on God's Word, He makes my way prosperous. (Josh. 1:8.)

7. I believe that nothing is impossible because I believe. (Mark 9:23.)

4 WAYS TO STAY INSPIRED

It doesn't take a lot of extra motivation to get excited at game time. But getting motivated for long practices or early mornings can seem like a long cross-country car ride. Here are 4 ways to stay inspired and make the journey to game time a little more scenic.

1. **Make each drill a competition.** If you have a teammate to compete against, work hard to push and stretch your skills during each phase of practice. If you are working on an individual part of your game, work on each task to better your personal best. Avoid simply going through the motions of practice. Practice doesn't make perfect; perfect practice makes perfect.

2. **Write down the goals you have in every area.** Don't just set goals for wins and losses, but set goals for speed, weight lifting, flexibility, and even

improvement in an area of weakness. As you write these down, you will begin to give yourself something to work toward in between major competitions.

3. **Post it.** Take the schedule for your upcoming season and post it in your locker or somewhere you go every day. Next to it, post your list of goals. As you see these each day, they will remind you of the things that you are working toward and making those sacrifices for.

4. **Stop and smell the roses.** Remember that no matter how serious you are, you started playing because you had a genuine interest and at some point along the way probably fell in love with the things involved in your sport. Don't lose sight of that fact; instead let it drive you to practice harder. Because you know that if you work hard, you will be better and more successful when game time arrives.

8 GOALS TO REACH BEFORE YOU'RE 18

At every stage in life, it is important to learn to set incremental goals towards the fulfillment of your dreams and vision. I encourage you to write down your goals as a regular reference point for your progress. Here are 8 goals to consider attaining before you're 18.

1. Make a long-term financial investment in the stock market.

2. Read the Bible through entirely.

3. Hold down one job for at least 6 months—a year if possible.

4. Read Dale Carnegie's book *How to Win Friends and Influence People*.

5. Obtain a basic idea of what career direction you are going to take, and make the necessary plans for school or training.

6. Develop one strong friendship that you will keep for life, no matter where you both end up.

7. Save enough money to buy a decent used car.

8. Keep your grades up, and get your high school diploma.

7 THINGS TO REMEMBER
WHEN STARTING OVER

Everyone has felt the need to start over with a clean slate more than once in their life. Here are some simple steps that will make starting over a success.

1. **Forgive yourself.** When we confess our sins to God, He forgives and cleanses us. (1 John 1:9.) David wrote in Psalm 103:12 that, "as far as the east is from the west, so far has He removed our transgressions from us." If God forgives and forgets our sins when we ask, we should also forgive ourselves. Sometimes we feel that if we mope around and punish ourselves for our sin that it will make us feel better. Jesus already took the punishment for our sin. You just need to receive God's forgiveness by faith and get on with your life.

2. **Learn from your mistake.** Did you get into this bad situation because of poor decisions in your friendships, entertainment choices, or wrong priorities? If you can identify the root cause, you can make changes to avoid this again in the future. Everyone makes mistakes, but to keep making the same one over is just plain stupid.

3. **Focus on your future, not your past.** Paul said, "…forgetting what is behind and straining toward what is ahead" (Phil. 3:13 NIV). You can't live in the present if you are always thinking about your past. You can't rewrite yesterday, but you can write a new story today.

4. **Build healthy relationships.** When starting over, it is good to evaluate if we have the healthy relationships we need. Healthy relationships will give the emotional and moral support you need to change and build over. Proverbs 27:17 (NIV) says, "As iron sharpens iron, so

one man sharpens another." Pick your friends care-fully. Look for ones that build you, believe in you, and back you up.

5. **Set yourself clear goals.** Proverbs 29:18 (KJV) says, "Where there is no vision, the people perish." If you aim at nothing, you will hit it every time. Nothing great was ever achieved without vision. Dream about what you want in your relationships, finances, career, and relationship with God.

6. **Put them in writing.** The Bible tells us in Habakkuk 2:2 to "Write the vision and make it plain on tablets, that he may run who reads it." Put your vision in writing and make it so clear that it gives you the momentum to run toward your dreams. Maybe you want to lose 10 pounds, or retire by 50 years old, or become a black belt. Whatever your goals, put them in writing and post them where you can see them every

day to help you run toward the things that really matter to you.

7. **Take steps.** Many of your goals may be long-term and seem hard to achieve. Don't try to take leaps toward your dreams, but rather take steps. Proverbs 20:24 says, "A man's steps are of the Lord." You don't eat a steak in one big bite—you eat it one bite at a time.

7 THINGS TALENT CANNOT DO

Talent can help you make the big play and get you spotted by the coaches, but there is a limit to what talent can do and how far it can take you. Taking time to develop the other parts of your game will help you succeed when you come across these 7 things that talent cannot do.

1. **Talent cannot make the right choices for you.** No matter what your talent level, when you hit tough choices, on and off the court, you have to make those choices just like everyone else.

2. **Talent cannot build team unity.** Team unity begins when each player knows that they are part of a whole. No matter how talented the individual is, no one can succeed alone.

3. **Talent cannot make your teammates better.**
   You have to work to make the people around you
   better. Elevating the game of your team takes time
   and patience.

4. **Talent cannot hustle.** Talent will fail in tough circumstances, but you can make those circumstances
   work in your favor by doing the things that don't show
   up on the stat sheet.

5. **Talent cannot teach you.** Taking the time to listen
   to those who have been where you are will help you
   take your game to the next level.

6. **Talent cannot keep you in shape.** In athletics,
   talent without physical conditioning is often worse
   than having no talent at all. Work hard to get in great
   shape, and your talent will shine even brighter.

7. **Talent cannot preserve your reputation.** The sports world is full of people who sacrificed their potential influence for temporary satisfaction. You will increase your influence if you use your talent the right way and choose a good reputation.

[TEAM]

4 QUALITIES OF A GREAT TEAMMATE

Ordinary teams become successful when individuals understand what it means to be a teammate. Here are 4 qualities that will help your team by helping you become an extraordinary teammate.

1. **Great teammates know their role.** Anything that has more than one part needs definition in order to be put together properly. If you don't know your role on a team, then you will never know if you are playing the right part or doing what it takes to play your part well.

2. **Great teammates take care of the responsibilities.** Once you know your role, work hard on your responsibilities in that role. You will earn the respect of your team and coaches as you prove that you will be where you are supposed to be and doing what you are supposed to be doing. Your team needs to know

that they can count on you to take care of your part while they are doing theirs.

3. **Great teammates make others look good.** If you only focus on your stats, your numbers, your percentages, or making yourself look good, you will quickly alienate your team and begin to lose their respect. Instead, look for ways to make your teammates look good at practice, at school, and during the game.

4. **Help your team improve by helping your teammates improve.** Working on your skills and ability may add to the effectiveness of your team, but working with your team to improve collectively will multiply your ability to produce great results. No matter what your skill level is right now, by helping the lesser players or pushing the greater players, you can help your team in some way.

3 THINGS TO DO IN AN INDIVIDUAL SPORT

Life seems individual in many ways, but our actions have a direct impact on those close to us. In golf, tennis, track and field, swimming, or any other individual sport, just as in life, when you seem to be isolated, there is always an extension of people who are affected by your competition. Here are 3 things you can do in an individual sport to create momentum for yourself as an individual athlete.

1. **Find a peer to practice with.** Work with your coach to find someone who is a small step better than you to practice with. Spend time with that person working on the fundamentals of your sport. While coaching is invaluable, there is a significant advantage when someone is performing a task with you or competing against you as you practice.

2. **Look for ways to compete above your current skill level.** Summer programs, public leagues, college camps, and open tournaments are great ways to continue improving and to learn new skills as you compete against players who have better times, averages, or experience than you. These challenges will help you elevate you game in preparation for upcoming seasons.

3. **Surround yourself with people who can give you advice.** Before, during, and after an event, consult with these coaches and advisors. By allowing others to help you prepare and perform, you place yourself in a team environment. No matter how isolated your sport, you will create an atmosphere of strength and support.

5 WAYS TO LEAD WITHOUT BEING A CAPTAIN

Leadership does not begin when you are given a title. It is a process that begins long before you are ever placed in a position or given official authority. These are 5 ways you can begin to lead now without being a captain.

1. **Support your coaches and team captains.** Anyone can be supportive when you win, but what are you doing and saying to support your team leaders during difficulty or when they aren't around? Your commitment to the team will show in what you do when something goes wrong or when a decision isn't popular.

2. **Volunteer for extra duties/assignments.** Be the first one to speak up when a special need is spotted or when your coach or captain needs an extra hand.

3. **Keep a positive attitude.** No matter how difficult a practice or how badly you are losing during a game, staying positive will help your teammates keep going. A positive attitude is contagious; unfortunately, so is a negative one.

4. **Lead by example.** Show up early, work hard, do things to the best of your ability, and be prepared when it's your turn to perform. Leading by example means doing what you would expect your coach or captain to do in the same circumstance.

5. **Go the extra mile to create team unity.** Think of ways to build relationships with the members of your team. Find time to get to know something about each person on your team. The better you know your team away from the game, the better you will know them when it comes time to play.

4 REASONS PEOPLE BECOME SELFISH

Have you ever wondered how someone could be so selfish? To answer that question and to help you avoid that same pitfall, here is a list of 4 reasons why people become selfish.

1. **They make the choice to be selfish.** We must make a decision not to be selfish, even if we don't feel like it. I have found that as you act on your decision, the feelings will come.

2. **They take for granted the joy of giving.** Not only will an unselfish act bring joy to others, but the giver will receive joy as well.

3. **They have unrenewed thinking.** We're all born naturally selfish, but that doesn't mean we must stay that way. We need to put selfless thoughts in and selfish thoughts out.

4. **They're unthankful.** Unthankfulness will cause people to become selfish. People who are unthankful stop recognizing the goodness of others; therefore, they develop an unwillingness to give.

6 WORDS HEARD IN A GREAT LOCKER ROOM

The way you talk about your team, your coach, your school, and your ability expresses your confidence in your talent and your confidence in the team. Great teams understand the importance of the words they speak. These are 6 words that you will hear in the locker room of every great team.

1. **"Dedication."** A great team is made up of individuals who are dedicated to the team and the goals of that team. No one is halfhearted or on the fence; everyone has bought into the system.

2. **"We."** When a conversation turns to taking credit or handing out blame, everyone knows that you win and lose as a team. Even the best players share the accolades and take the heat with everyone else.

3. **"Yes, sir."** An understanding of authority and a respect for leadership is one of the largest components of a winning team. The individuals in a great locker room show that respect in the way they respond and communicate with coaches and team leaders.

4. **"Can."** No matter what the circumstance, players in a great locker room keep hope alive with the words they say. You will never hear them say that they think something is impossible or that a goal is out of reach. Each player will stay positive until the final whistle.

5. **"Please."** Manners, etiquette, and protocol are important details in a great locker room. Each player must have mutual respect for the talent, ideals, and property of everyone else.

6. **"Good job."** Players in this environment are always quick to offer congratulations on a job well done.

Supporting each other with words of encouragement and affirmation are vital to creating team spirit.

[GAME DAY]

3 THINGS TO AVOID THE NIGHT BEFORE

Everyone has a game day tradition. You might wear your jersey to class, show up 4 hours early to the field house, or wear 4 pairs of striped socks. No matter what your game day traditions, here are 3 things to avoid the night before to make sure that you get there at 100%.

1. **Avoid staying up late.** Sleep is one of the few things that you can't grab at the corner store on the way to the game. It can be tempting to hang out with friends or watch a movie, but make the effort to get to bed at a good time. You will be glad you did at game time.

2. **Avoid foods that cause dehydration.** Certain foods, especially drinks with caffeine, can cause your body to try and eliminate valuable fluids. Avoiding

these as well as foods that are difficult to digest will help keep you from feeling sluggish on game day.

3. **Avoid unnecessary busyness.** While there are things that you have to address, such as homework, cutting out the unnecessary tasks will help you lower your stress level and focus on the game.

5 WAYS TO STOP THE BUTTERFLIES

While everyone gets pre-game jitters, great players know how to turn those butterflies into excitement and steer clear of anxiety. Use these 5 ways to stop the butterflies and come out of the locker room ready to perform.

1. **Get ready early.** If you can, take care of the details early so you can take time to think about the game. You can avoid a big part of the butterflies by not feeling hurried.

2. **Find a quiet area to get your thoughts on the game.** The less extra noise you have to filter, the more you can feel focused on the game.

3. **Write down your key game plan points before the game day.** Pull these out prior to the game, and spend some time looking over them as a reminder. The

more prepared you feel, the less you will have to get anxious about. Fear grows when you are worried about the unknown.

4. **Take nervous energy and make it positive energy.** Stretching and warming up are the 2 best ways to get your blood flowing and to translate the psychological energy into physical effectiveness.

5. **Relax!** The feelings of game day are one of the best aspects of playing sports. It would be incredibly boring to play without the emotions. So enjoy the excitement, but don't let it turn to anxiety and rob you of the experience of competition.

3 BELIEFS YOU MUST HAVE TO WIN

Beliefs in sports are just as important as practice and conditioning. If you do not have the right personal beliefs, you are already beaten before you ever step onto the playing surface. If you want to win, you must believe these 3 things.

1. **"We will win."** Of course you know that everyone will lose from time to time. But if you don't believe that you can win every time out, then you have already given your opponent an advantage long before you face them in competition.

2. **"I can do my part."** Believe that you can and will do what your position requires. Whether as a star or a role player, you must know that you can step up when you are called upon to perform.

3. **"Our game plan will work."** You, and your team, have to believe in the game plan your coaches set up for you. If you don't believe in it going into the game, it is doomed to fail and you will be hesitant to act on it as you compete.

4 THINGS TO REMEMBER
WHEN YOU'RE LOSING

From time to time, you will find yourself in a situation that no one likes: losing. In these moments, great athletes separate themselves by their response to adversity. You may not always respond by turning the tables and creating a win, but your character will shine bright if you remember 4 things.

1. **Other comebacks have been made.** You are not the first team to be trailing during a competition. Remind yourself of some of those great comebacks and keep playing.

2. **Take it one play at a time.** Unless you have one last chance to win the game, you can't come back and win all in one play. Take it one play at a time, and take those small steps toward winning.

3. **Don't play halfway.** Habits are built during every competition. If you wouldn't play that way while you're winning, don't play that way while you're losing. Show respect to everyone involved by finishing strong, no matter what the final outcome.

4. **It's not over yet.** As long as there is time left, believe that you have a chance to win. Set a small goal to reach, then as you reach those smaller goals, set another and then another. Put all your effort into completing the comeback, and never, ever give up.

3 MARKS OF A WINNER

Winners are easily spotted by the results of their performance, but it is the things that are done before the results are visible that truly mark someone for greatness. These are 3 characteristics of success that mark a winner.

1. **A winner sets the pace.** The winner is the one who is doing things the right way, and doing them the right way before it is the popular thing to do. A winner puts in the time and energy to succeed, plans ahead, and works past obstacles before anyone asks. They are out in front, leading by example.

2. **A winner always gives 100%.** Even when talent alone could be enough to carry them to victory, the winner is the one who works the hardest to be their best.

3. **A winner works with the team.** At times the chance to be excluded from the team is available, but a mark of a true winner is the choice to work with the team and take glory and blame as a part of the whole. A winner sees the team as the most valuable and will do anything they can to help other teammates grow and succeed.

[SPORTSMANSHIP]

3 THINGS TO DO RIGHT AFTER A LOSS

Emotions can be heated right after you lose, but your response to setback will help determine your future effectiveness. Doing these 3 things right after you lose will help you recover quickly and show class even in defeat.

1. **Congratulate your opponent.** Show character and respect for the other team by rising about your negative emotions for a moment just after the game is done. You show great poise by fighting the temptation to storm off the field or demonstrate anger.

2. **Write down the things that you would have done differently.** Take the loss as a learning experience. Listen to your coach, and find the areas that you can work on or correct for next time. Many athletes are so angry after a loss that they miss the

chance to improve, and they end up repeating the

same mistakes again.

3. **Set your sights on the next goal.** Whether it is

your next practice or the next game, begin the process

of overcoming the loss by focusing on what you can

change instead of overanalyzing what you can't. Begin

to focus on the next competition.

3 THINGS TO DO RIGHT AFTER A WIN

Winning can make everything seem perfect, but what you do in the post-game will determine your team growth after a victory. These 3 things will help you build momentum if you do them right after you win.

1. **Congratulate your opponent.** After you win, it can be easy to forget that your opponent just lost. Take a moment to demonstrate character and show respect to your opponent by acknowledging them in a positive way.

2. **Share the wealth.** Your success is due to the efforts of the whole team. Take this opportunity to share words of encouragement with your teammates. Team unity is built by sharing the joy of each victory.

3. **Take notes on the things you would have done differently.** Even though you just won, it is important to acknowledge the things that can be improved. Realize that the single victory is not the ultimate prize and there is more to work towards in the games to come.

3 THINGS TO DO RIGHT AFTER A TIE

Every now and then, you may come across a situation when you tie in competition. Even though it is not a loss and not a win, the things you do following the game will help you grow as a player and a team after a tie.

1. **Congratulate your opponent.** You didn't lose, but neither did they. Taking time to show sportsmanship demonstrates character and respect for the efforts that your opponent gave during competition.

2. **Do what you would have done after a loss.** The game might not go in the loss column, but you didn't win either. The goal of the competition is to win. If you come short of the prize, find the things that you need to improve to change the outcome next time.

3. **Treat your teammates the way you would if you won.** Building off of the positive aspects as a team is just as important as fixing the things that kept you from winning the game. Stay positive with your words and attitude towards your teammates.

7 REASONS NOT TO BECOME A GOOD LOSER

Losing is not the end of the world, but no one likes the feelings that accompany defeat. While you want to be a good sport, here are 7 reasons not to become a good loser.

1. **Losing is not the point.** The goal is to win. No matter what happened in the last game, you should compete to win every time you play.

2. **Getting comfortable with losing robs you of your hunger to win.** If you feel okay with losing, you will probably lose more often than you win.

3. **"It's how you play the game."** People often say this to downplay winning and spare the feelings of those who lost. But playing the game the right way is important. You cannot play the game the right way without playing to win.

4. **Feeling like everything is going to be the same if you win or lose helps you become lazy.** There are few things as destructive to a team as laziness.

5. **Lazy athletes are more likely to get injured.** When you play halfheartedly, you set yourself up to be out of position and subject yourself to injury.

6. **Lazy athletes are more likely to lose playing time to a more aggressive teammate.** If you want to sit on the bench, the quickest way to get there is to stop caring about winning.

7. **Successful habits are developed as you strive to win by succeeding one play at a time.** Winning or losing is not something that happens all at once; it is determined by your success on each play. If you stop caring about winning, you begin to lose the passion to succeed on each play.

4 WAYS TO KEEP THE FUN IN SPORTS

If you are like most people, you began to play sports because you enjoyed the experience. As you moved to each new level of competition, the sport became more and more about winning. There might be a big prize to play for, but if you don't enjoy the ride, it is somewhat pointless to continue. So here are 4 ways to keep the fun in your sport and enjoy every step of the journey.

1. **Remember why you started playing.** Don't lose sight of how much excitement you have when you play and compete.

2. **Take time off.** If you don't ever take time to relax away from your passions, they can become over-whelming. It is hard to enjoy something that feels hard to undertake.

3. **Enjoy the success of others.** As you celebrate the success of your teammates and plug into the results and the efforts of others, your excitement multiplies. You begin to create an atmosphere of anticipation every time you compete.

4. **Set rewards for reaching your goals.** If you have nothing to look forward to, you probably won't be excited just for the sake of being excited. Decide before the season what you will do if you reach the next goal. The payoff can be large or small. The idea is simply that you give yourself a bigger reward to look forward to than a pat on the back. As you do these things, you will find that you keep the passion of competing alive and well!

PRAYER OF SALVATION

God loves you—no matter who you are, no matter what your past. God loves you so much that He gave His one and only begotten Son for you. The Bible tells us that "...whoever believes in him shall not perish but have eternal life" (John 3:16 NIV). Jesus laid down His life and rose again so that we could spend eternity with Him in heaven and experience His absolute best on earth. If you would like to receive Jesus into your life, say the following prayer out loud and mean it from your heart.

Heavenly Father, I come to You admitting that I am a sinner. Right now, I choose to turn away from sin, and I ask You to cleanse me of all unrighteousness. I believe that Your Son, Jesus, died on the cross to take away my sins. I also believe that He rose again from the dead so that I might be forgiven of my sins and made righteous through faith in Him. I call upon the name of Jesus Christ to be the Savior and Lord of my life. Jesus, I choose to follow You and ask that You fill me with the power of the Holy Spirit. I declare that right now I am a child of God. I am free from sin and full of the righteousness of God. I am saved in Jesus' name. Amen.

If you prayed this prayer to receive Jesus Christ as your Savior for the first time, please contact us on the Web at **www.harrisonhouse.com** to receive a free book.

Or you may write to us at:

Harrison House

P.O. Box 35035

Tulsa, Oklahoma 74153

ABOUT THE AUTHOR

Blaine Bartel founded Thrive Communications, an organization dedicated to serving those who shape the local church. He is also currently leading a new church launch in a growing area of north Dallas.

Bartel was the founding youth pastor and one of the key strategists in the creation of Oneighty, which has become one of the most emulated youth ministries in the past decade reaching 2,500 – 3,000 students weekly under his leadership. In a tribute to the long term effects and influence of Blaine's leadership, hundreds of young people that grew up under his ministry are now serving in full time ministry themselves.

A recognized authority on the topics of youth ministry and successful parenting, Bartel is a best-selling author with 12 books published in 4 languages, and is the creator of Thrive—one of the most listened to youth ministry development systems in the country, selling more than 100,000 audio tapes and CD's worldwide. He is one of the most sought after speakers in his field; more than one million people from over 40 countries have attended Blaine Bartel's live seminars or speaking engagements.

His work has been featured in major media including "The Washington Post," CBS' "The Early Show," "The 700 Club," "Seventeen" magazine, as well as newspapers, radio programs, and Internet media worldwide.

Bartel's commitment to creating an enduring legacy that will impact the world is surpassed only by his passion for family as a dedicated father of three children and a loving husband to his wife of more than 20 years, Cathy.

To contact Blaine Bartel,

write:

Blaine Bartel

Serving America's Future

P.O. Box 691923

Tulsa, OK 74169

Or visit him on his Web site at:

www.blainebartel.com

To contact Oneighty®, write:

Oneighty®

P.O. Box 770

Tulsa, OK 74101

www.Oneighty.com

OTHER BOOKS BY BLAINE BARTEL

every teenager's
Little Black Book
on reaching your dreams

every teenager's
Little Black Book
on how to get along with your parents

every teenager's
Little Black Book
of God's guarantees

every teenager's
Little Black Book
on how to win a friend to Christ

every teenager's
Little Black Book
on cash

every teenager's
Little Black Book
on cool

every teenager's
Little Black Book
on sex and dating

every teenager's
Little Black Book
of hard to find information

Little Black Book
for graduates

Thrive Teen Devotional

The Big Black Book
for parents

Let Me Tell You What
Your Teens Are Telling Me

7 Absolutes to Pray Over Your Kids

For more information on the *little black book* series
please visit our website at: **www.littleblackbooks.info**

Available at fine bookstores everywhere
or at **www.harrisonhouse.com**

Take the Turn for God in Just 5 Minutes a Day

Witty, short, and inspiring devotions for teens from one of America's youth leadership specialists!

Teens can discover a real, action-packed, enthusiastic relationship with God. The thrive.teen.devotional is motivated by a very simple challenge: Give just five minutes a day to God and watch your life turn around.

At the end of eight weeks, the Word of God is going to be more real and alive to teens than ever before as they gain spiritual insights on issues like friendships, self-esteem, and prayer. The good news is that when one's mind is renewed, they experience a radical turnaround in every other area of their life, too.

thrive.teen.devotional
by Blaine Bartel
1-57794-777-0

Fast. Easy.
Convenient.

THE HARRISON HOUSE VISION

Proclaiming the truth and the power

Of the Gospel of Jesus Christ

With excellence;

Challenging Christians to

Live victoriously,

Grow spiritually,

Know God intimately.